Christmas

THE FATHER'S GIFT

BILLY GRAHAM

THOMAS NELSON
Since 1798

NASHVILLE   DALLAS   MEXICO CITY   RIO DE JANEIRO   BEIJING

Christmas: The Father's Gift

Copyright © 2008 by Thomas Nelson Publishers, Inc.

Published in Nashville, Tennessee, by Thomas Nelson, Inc.

Thomas Nelson, Inc. titles may be purchased in bulk for educational, business, fundraising, or sales promotional use. For information, please e-mail SpecialMarkets@ThomasNelson.com.

Portions of this book were excerpted from *This Christmas Night* by Billy and Ruth Graham © 2007. Used by permission.

The poem "But You" was taken from *Ruth Bell Graham's Collected Poems*, ©1977, 1992, 1997. Used by permission.

Unless otherwise indicated, all Scripture quotations in this book are from the *New King James Version* © 1979, 1980, 1992, 2002 Thomas Nelson, Inc., Publisher and are used by permission. Other Scripture references are from the *King James Version* (KJV).

Designed by Robin Black, www.blackbirdcreative.biz

ISBN-13: 978-1-4041-8736-8
ISBN-10: 1-4041-8736-7

www.thomasnelson.com

Printed in Canada

FOREWORD

*C*hristmas is the most thrilling season of the year. As we look back over the years, memories of many Christmases flood our minds. Christmas cards that we read and reread, the smell of pine drifting through the house, the fireplace crackling—all of these things turn our thoughts to those we love.

Ruth and I treasured these moments spent with family and friends each year as we gathered to celebrate the Christmas message: a message of hope and joy and love.

But Christmas means something far deeper than human good will. It is the loving remembrance of the birth of the Savior. Over two thousand years ago, on a night the world has come to call Christmas, a young Jewish maiden went through the experience countless mothers had before her, and would since: She brought forth a child. But this was no

3

ordinary child. This was the unique Son of God, sent from Heaven to save us from our sins (Matthew 1:21).

Amid the glitter and busyness of the season, may you not lose sight of the miracle and meaning of that Christmas night. With the shepherds and the wise men, let us fall down and worship Him!

BILLY GRAHAM

THE GIFT OF
Hope

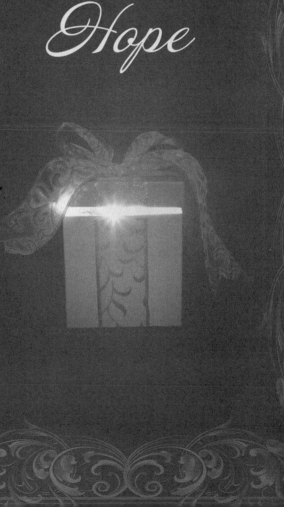

$\mathcal{C}$hristmas is not just a date on the calendar. It is the celebration of the event that set Heaven to singing, an event that gave the stars of the night sky a new brilliance. The Hebrew prophets believed that God had made the world. But all through the centuries they seem to have been saying,

"I wish that God would become personal." And through the centuries God gave them the assurance that He would.

This is precisely what He did that first Christmas night. He became personal in Bethlehem. "The Word became flesh and dwelt among us" (John 1:14). At a specific time and at a specific place a specific person was born—and that Person was God of very God, the Lord Jesus Christ. What a wonderful and glorious hope we have because of that first Christmas!

The King is Promised

Eight hundred years before the birth of Christ, the prophet Isaiah declared: "The people who walked in darkness have seen a great light" (Isaiah 9:2). It was the promise of the coming of Christ and the light that was to dawn upon the world. It heralded the entrance of God into human history. It promised Heaven descending to earth. It was as though a trumpeter had taken his stand upon the turrets of time and announced to a despairing, hopeless, and frustrated world the coming of the Prince of Peace.

Unto Us

The people who walked in darkness
  Have seen a great light;
  Those who dwelt in the land of the
    shadow of death,
  Upon them a light has shined.

For unto us a Child is born,
  Unto us a Son is given;
  And the government will be upon His shoulder.
  And His name will be called
  Wonderful, Counselor, Mighty God,
  Everlasting Father, Prince of Peace.
    Of the increase of His government
      and peace
  There will be no end,
  Upon the throne of David and over His
    kingdom,
  To order it and establish it with judgment
    and justice
  From that time forward, even forever.
  The zeal of the Lord of hosts will perform this.

ISAIAH 9:2, 6–7

O Come, O Come, Emmanuel

O come, O come, Emmanuel,
And ransom captive Israel,
That mourns in lonely exile here
Until the Son of God appear
Rejoice! Rejoice! Emmanuel
Shall come to thee, O Israel.

O come, Thou Day-Spring, come and cheer
Our spirits by Thine advent here
Disperse the gloomy clouds of night,
And death's dark shadows put to flight.
Rejoice! Rejoice! Emmanuel
Shall come to thee, O Israel.

O come, Thou Key of David, come,
And open wide our heavenly home;
Make safe the way that leads on high,
And close the path to misery.
Rejoice! Rejoice! Emmanuel
Shall come to thee, O Israel.

LATIN, 12TH CENTURY

9

The Angelic Announcement to Mary

Now in the sixth month the angel Gabriel was sent by God to a city of Galilee named Nazareth, to a virgin betrothed to a man whose name was Joseph, of the house of David. The virgin's name was Mary. And having come in, the angel said to her, "Rejoice, highly favored one, the Lord is with you; blessed are you among women!"

But when she saw him, she was troubled at his saying, and considered what manner of greeting this was. Then the angel said to her, "Do not be afraid, Mary, for you have found favor with God. And behold, you will conceive in your womb and bring forth a Son, and shall call His name JESUS. He will be great, and will be called the Son of the Highest; and the Lord God will give Him the throne of His father David. And He will reign over the house of Jacob forever, and of His kingdom there will be no end."

Then Mary said to the angel, "How can this be, since I do not know a man?"

And the angel answered and said to her,
"The Holy Spirit will come upon you, and the
power of the Highest will overshadow you;
therefore, also, that Holy One who is to be born
will be called the Son of God. Now indeed,
Elizabeth your relative has also conceived a son
in her old age; and this is now the sixth month
for her who was called barren. For with God
nothing will be impossible. Then Mary said,
'Behold the maidservant of the Lord! Let it be to
me according to your word.' And the angel
departed from her."

LUKE 1:26–38

One evening in Jerusalem I looked out my
hotel window and saw the lights of Bethlehem
in the distance. For a long time I stood there
and meditated on the events that had taken
place over 2,000 years ago and which have
transformed and changed our world.

I thought about the angel Gabriel. He
came to Mary, who was no more than a

teenager, and said, "Do not be afraid, Mary, for you have found favor with God. And behold, you will conceive in your womb and bring forth a Son, and shall call His name JESUS" (Luke 1:30–31).

At first Mary was fearful and deeply disturbed. Here she was, a virgin, engaged to a godly man by the name of Joseph, yet she was to be made pregnant supernaturally by the Holy Spirit. People would talk, shame could be attached to it, and Joseph might even reject her. But Mary by faith said, "Behold the maidservant of the Lord! Let it be to me according to your word" (Luke 1:38). One of the greatest demonstrations of faith in all the Bible was Mary's answer to the angel, accepting God's will for her life—no matter the cost.

God's Assurance to
Joseph

*N*ow the birth of Jesus Christ was as follows: After His mother Mary was betrothed to Joseph, before they came together, she was found with child of the Holy Spirit. Then Joseph her husband, being a just man, and not wanting to make her a public example, was minded to put her away secretly. But while he thought about these things, behold, an angel of the Lord appeared to him in a dream, saying, "Joseph, son of David, do not be afraid to take to you Mary your wife, for that which is conceived in her is of the Holy Spirit. And she will bring forth a Son, and you shall call His name JESUS, for He will save His people from their sins."

So all this was done that it might be fulfilled which was spoken by the Lord through the prophet, saying: "Behold, the virgin shall be with child, and bear a Son, and they shall call His name Immanuel," which is translated, "God with us." Then Joseph, being aroused from

*sleep, did as the angel of the Lord commanded
him and took to him his wife...*

MATTHEW 1:18–24

In the Scriptures we are given just a little
glimpse of Mary and Joseph before Jesus was
born. They lived in the hill country of Galilee.
Joseph was a religious man, and Mary gives
every evidence of a thorough knowledge of the
Scriptures, even though she was just a teenager.

Joseph was contracted to marry Mary,
and in that time, being engaged was almost as
strong a commitment as being married. I think
we give too little attention to Joseph. He is
called "a just man" (Matthew 1:19), which
means he obeyed the will of God. It also
includes the connotation of sympathy and
kindness. It indicated his devotion both to
God and to Mary.

Then Mary was found to be with child.
Put yourself in Joseph's place. Imagine his
thoughts, his suspicions, about the girl to

whom he was engaged. According to the ancient law, Mary should have been put to death. But Joseph did not want to have any part of that kind of punishment, so he decided to break the engagement privately.

While he as thinking about these things, God's angel appeared to him in a dream to give the prospective bridegroom an explanation of the situation. "Joseph, son of David," said the angel, "do not be afraid to take to you Mary your wife, for that which is conceived in her is of the Holy Spirit" (Matthew 1:20).

What faith it took on Joseph's part to believe that message and to trust! He put away his suspicions. He believed God and was married to Mary. Like Mary, he said, "Yes, Lord, regardless!"

THE GIFT OF
Joy

The Wondrous Birth
of Jesus Christ

And it came to pass in those days that a decree went out from Caesar Augustus that all the world should be registered. This census first took place while Quirinius was governing Syria. So all went to be registered, everyone to his own city.

Joseph also went up from Galilee, out of the city of Nazareth, into Judea, to the city of David, which is called Bethlehem, because he was of the house and lineage of David, to be registered with Mary, his betrothed wife, who was with child. So it was, that while they were there, the days were completed for her to be delivered. And she brought forth her firstborn Son, and wrapped Him in swaddling cloths, and laid Him in a manger, because there was no room for them in the inn.

LUKE 2:1–7

Among the most tragic words ever penned are those found in Luke's account of the first Christmas. "There was no room for them in the inn." There was room for merchants, tax collectors, travelers and sightseers, but no room for the gentle Mary and the divine Christ, who was to be born that night.

What was the cause of this tragedy? Why was there no room for Mary and Joseph and their expected Baby, except in a stable? I have some sympathy for the innkeeper. He was not hostile; he was not opposed to the couple; but his inn was crowded; his hands were full; his mind was preoccupied. After all, it was an unusually busy time, with guests arriving from every corner of Israel for the census and taxation. He probably told Joseph, "I wish I could help you, but I must keep my priorities. But I'm not a hardhearted man. Over there is the stable. You are welcome to use it if you care to, but that is the best I can do. Now I must get back to my work."

No room for Jesus? No room for the King of kings? This is the answer that millions are giving today. It is the answer of preoccupation—not fierce opposition, not furious hatred, but unconcern about spiritual things.

Things have not really changed since that Bethlehem night two thousand years ago. God is still on the fringes of most of our lives. We fit Him in when it is convenient for us, but we become irritated when He makes demands on us. Our lives are so full. There is so much to be done. But in all our busy activities are we in danger of excluding from our hearts and lives the One who made us?

O Little Town of Bethlehem

O little town of Bethlehem,
How still we see thee lie!
Above thy deep and dreamless sleep
The silent stars go by.
Yet in thy dark streets shineth
The everlasting Light;
The hopes and fears of all the years
Are met in thee tonight

For Christ is born of Mary,
And gathered all above,
While mortals sleep, the angels keep
Their watch of wondering love.
O morning stars, together,
Proclaim the holy birth!
And praises sing to God the King,
And peace to men on earth!

How silently, how silently,
The wondrous gift is given;
So God imparts to human hearts

The blessings of His heaven.
No ear may hear His coming,
But in this world of sin,
Where meek souls will receive Him still,
The dear Christ enters in.

O holy Child of Bethlehem
Descend to us, we pray
Cast out our sin and enter in,
Be born to us today
We hear the Christmas angels,
The great glad tidings tell;
O come to us, abide with us,
Our Lord Emmanuel!

PHILIP BROOKS, 1868

THE WORLD'S HOLIEST NIGHT

"But you, Bethlehem Ephrathah,
Though you are little among the thousands of Judah,
Yet out of you shall come forth to Me
The One to be Ruler in Israel,
Whose goings forth are from of old,
From everlasting."
And He shall stand and feed His flock
In the strength of the LORD,
In the majesty of the name of the LORD His God;
And they shall abide,
For now He shall be great
To the ends of the earth;
And this One shall be peace."

MICAH 5:2, 4–5a

Imagine the scene in Bethlehem. It was the
night of nights, and yet it had begun as every
other night had before it. In Bethlehem's
houses mothers lay their children down to
sleep. In the courtyards of the inn some camels
lay down to rest. In the fields the sheep lay
down while the shepherds sat near their fires.
In the heavens above appeared the same stars
that had shined throughout all the ages, ever
since God had made the stars to rule by night.

Here in the dark cave, as a flickering torch casts high shadows of long-horned oxen on the rough-hewn logs, there is no sound but the munching of hay by the cattle. In the midst lies the young mother, forgetting for the moment her discomfort, for in her arms lies the Babe, her baby boy.

Who would dream that He is the King of kings and Lord of lords? Those chubby little hands that clasped the straw in His manger crib were soon to open blinded eyes, unstop deaf ears, and still the troubled seas. That cooing voice was soon to be lifted to command demons to depart, to teach men of the Way, and to raise the dead. Those tiny feet were to take Him to the sick and needy and were finally to be pierced on Calvary's Cross.

That manger crib in remote Bethlehem became the link that bound a lost world to a loving God. From that manger came a Man who not only taught us a new way of life, but brought us into a new relationship with our Creator.

Joy to the World

Joy to the world! The Lord is come!
Let earth receive her King;
Let every heart prepare Him room,
And heaven and nature sing,
And heaven and nature sing,
And heaven, and heaven, and nature sing.

Joy to the world the Savior reigns!
Let men their songs employ,
While fields and floods, rocks, hills, and plains
Repeat the sounding joy,
Repeat the sounding joy,
Repeat, repeat, the sounding joy.

No more let sins and sorrows grow,
Nor thorns infest the ground;
He comes to make His blessings flow
Far as the curse is found,
Far as the curse is found,
Far as, far as, the curse is found.

He rules the world with truth and grace,
And makes the nations prove
The glories of His righteousness,
And wonders of His love,
And wonders of His love,
And wonders, and wonders, of His love.

ISAAC WATTS, 1674–1748

HEAVEN AND EARTH REJOICE

Now there were in the same country shepherds living out in the fields, keeping watch over their flock by night. And behold, an angel of the Lord stood before them, and the glory of the Lord shone around them, and they were greatly afraid. Then the angel said to them, "Do not be afraid, for behold, I bring you good tidings of great joy which will be to all people. For there is born to you this day in the city of David a Savior, who is Christ the Lord. And this will be the sign to you: You will find a Babe wrapped in swaddling cloths, lying in a manger."

*And suddenly there was with the angel
a multitude of the heavenly host praising God
and saying:*

*"Glory to God in the highest,
And on earth peace, goodwill toward men!"*

*So it was, when the angels had gone away
from them into heaven, that the shepherds said
to one another, "Let us now go to Bethlehem
and see this thing that has come to pass, which
the Lord has made known to us." And they
came with haste and found Mary and Joseph,
and the Babe lying in a manger. Now when
they had seen Him, they made widely known
the saying which was told them concerning this
Child. And all those who heard it marveled at
those things which were told them by the
shepherds. But Mary kept all these things and
pondered them in her heart. Then the shepherds
returned, glorifying and praising God for all the
things that they had heard and seen, as it was
told them.*

LUKE 2:8–20

The stars shone like diamonds in the cold, crisp sky. On the hills outside the little village of Bethlehem the flocks had been gathered, and watch was being kept to protect them from the constant threat of roving wolves or marauding bandits.

Like most of the people of Palestine, those shepherds outside Bethlehem were poor and insignificant men. They had no reason to expect that this night would be different from any other. But God had other plans. This was the night when God Himself would come to earth. The dull routine of their lives was suddenly and dramatically shattered by the appearance of the angels, and the tidings of Christ's birth echoed across the skies.

What is the message of those Christmas angels? First of all, it is a message of love and peace. "Glory to God in the highest, and on earth peace, good will toward men," sang the angelic multitude (Luke 2:14). It is a message of joy and hope. "Behold, I bring you good

tidings of great joy, which shall be to all people"
(Luke 2:10). The message of the Christmas
angels is that God not only exists, but that
He is a loving heavenly Father who seeks to
restore us to what we were created to be—His
children. Because God's Son, Jesus Christ, has
entered this world, we know beyond a shadow
of doubt that joy and hope can be ours if we
will but receive the gift of Christmas.

It Came Upon the Midnight Clear

It came upon the midnight clear,
That glorious song of old,
From angels bending near the earth,
To touch their harps of gold;
"Peace on the earth, good will to men,
From Heaven's all gracious King."
The world in solemn stillness lay,
To hear the angels sing.

And ye, beneath life's crushing load,
Whose forms are bending low,
Who toil along the climbing way

With painful steps and slow,
Look now! for glad and golden hours
Come swiftly on the wing.
O rest beside the weary road,
And hear the angels sing!

For lo! the days are hastening on,
By prophet-bards foretold,
When with the ever-circling years
Comes round the age of gold;
When peace shall over all the earth
Its ancient splendors fling,
And the whole world sends back the song
Which now the angels sing.

THE GIFT OF

Love

The Worship of the Wise Men

Now after Jesus was born in Bethlehem in Judea in the days of Herod the king, behold, wise men from the east came to Jerusalem, saying, "Where is He who has been born King of the Jews? For we have seen His star in the East and have come to worship him." When Herod the king heard this, he was troubled, and all Jerusalem with him. And when he had gathered all the chief priests and scribes of the people together, he inquired of them where the Christ was to be born.

So they said to him, "In Bethlehem of Judea, for thus it is written by the prophet: 'But you, Bethlehem, in the land of Judah, are not the least among the rulers of Judah; for out of you will come a ruler who will shepherd My people Israel.'"

Then Herod when he had secretly called the wise men, determined from them what time the star appeared. And he sent them to Bethlehem and said, "Go and search carefully for the young Child.

And when you have found Him, bring back word to me, that I may come and worship Him also."

After they had heard the king, they departed, and behold, the star which they had seen in the East went before them, till it came and stood over where the young Child was. When they saw the star they rejoiced with exceedingly great joy.

And when they had come into the house, they saw the young Child with Mary His mother, and fell down and worshiped Him. And when they had opened their treasures, they presented gifts to Him: gold, frankincense, and myrrh. And having been divinely warned in a dream that they should not return to Herod, they departed for their own country another way.

MATTHEW 2:1–12

On Christmas day, when our children were little, they would awaken before daylight, their eyes dancing with expectation to open the gifts. Before we opened the gifts, we read the Bible and prayed. What a thrill it was to celebrate the birthday of God's Son, Jesus Christ.

One of the passages that we read was from the Gospel of Matthew, where the wise men came from the East to Jerusalem, following a star. They came to the house of Joseph, fell down and worshiped the Christ Child, and "presented unto him gifts; gold, frankincense, and myrrh" (Matthew 2:11b).

Every year people write me saying how much they dread Christmas. Often their complaint stems from how busy they will be, or how much money they will spend. Did those wise men who journeyed hundreds of miles across the desert to seek out the infant Jesus ever feel that way? After all, it took months to make the arduous trip, and they had gone to great expense to provide gifts of gold, frankincense, and myrrh for the new child.

I doubt it. In fact, as their journey neared its end we read they had "exceedingly great joy" (v 10). What made the difference? Their focus was totally on Jesus, the One who would be called "Immanuel...God with us" (Matthew 1:23).

Don't let this Christmas season overwhelm

you. Don't feel you have to do everything, or go into debt just to impress other people. Focus instead on Jesus. Make this Christmas one of "exceedingly great joy"!

God Himself Is with Us

In the beginning was the Word, and the Word was with God, and the Word was God. He was in the beginning with God. All things were made through Him, and without Him nothing was made that was made.

And the Word became flesh and dwelt among us, and we beheld His glory, the glory as of the only begotten of the Father, full of grace and truth.

JOHN 1:1–3, 14

Sometimes in the rush of Christmas activity we forget that the most wondrous part of Christmas is the fact that in the person of Jesus Christ, God became flesh in order to save us from our sins. This is the crux and the core of the Christian message.

The prophets wrote of it, the Psalmists sang

of it, the apostles rejoiced and built their hopes on it, and the Epistles are filled with it. Christ's coming in the flesh—His invading the world, His identifying Himself with sinful men and women—is the most significant fact of history.

What an incredible truth! Think of it: The God of the universe came down from Heaven that first Christmas night and took human form! If you want to know what God is like, then take a long look at Jesus Christ—because He was God in human flesh. In Him were displayed not only the perfections that had been exhibited in the creation—such as wisdom, power and majesty—but also such perfections as justice, mercy, grace and love. "The Word was God…And the Word was made flesh and dwelt among us" (John 1:1, 14).

To His disciples Jesus said, "You believe in God, believe also in Me" (John 14:1). This sequence of faith is inevitable. If we believe in what God made and what God said, we will believe in the One whom God sent.

HARK! THE HERALD ANGELS SING

Hark! the herald angels sing,
Glory to the new-born King,
Peace on earth and mercy mild,
God and sinner reconcil'ed.
Joyful, all ye nations, rise,
Join the triumph of the skies;
With the angelic host proclaim,
"Christ is born in Bethlehem".

Hark! the herald angels sing,
"Glory to the new-born King".

Christ by highest heaven ador'ed,
Christ, the everlasting Lord!
Late in time behold Him come,
Offspring of a Virgin's womb,
Veiled in flesh the God-head see,
Hail the incarnate Deity!
Pleased in flesh with us to dwell,
Jesus our Immanuel.

Hail the Heaven-born Prince of Peace!
Hail the Sun of righteousness!
Light and life to all He brings,
Risen with healing in His wings.
Mild He lays His glory by,
Born that we no more may die,
Born to raise us from the earth,
Born to give us second birth.

CHARLES WESLEY, 1739

THE GIFT OF

Peace

PEACE IN THE MIDST OF THE STORM

"Peace I leave with you. My peace I give to you; not as the world gives do I give to you. Let not your heart be troubled, neither let it be afraid."

"These things I have spoken to you, that in Me you may have peace. In the world you will have tribulation; but be of good cheer, I have overcome the world."

JOHN 14:27; 16:33

Once, during the First World War, on Christmas Eve, the battlefield was strangely quiet. As the soft snow fell, the thoughts of the young men were of home and their families. Softly one lad began to hum "Silent Night". Wheezy tenors and throaty baritones took up the chorus until the trenches resounded with the Christmas song. When they finished singing, they were astonished to hear the song echoing from the trenches across no-man's-land: In their own tongue the other soldiers also sang "Silent Night". That night they all were thinking of the Prince of Peace, the Christ of Christmas.

How different this world would be if we could unite together around that "Holy Infant so tender and mild!" And it can happen as we open our hearts and lives to Jesus Christ, the Prince of Peace.

SILENT NIGHT

Silent Night! Holy Night!
All is calm, all is bright.
Round yon virgin mother and child!
Holy Infant so tender and mild,
sleep in heavenly peace, sleep in
　　heavenly peace!

Silent night! Holy night!
Shepherds quake at the sight;
glories stream from heaven afar;
heav'nly hosts sing alleluia –
Christ the Savior is born! Christ the Savior
　　is born!

Silent night! Holy night!
Son of God, love's pure light
radiant beams from Thy holy face
with the dawn of redeeming grace –
Jesus, Lord at Thy birth, Jesus, Lord
　　at Thy birth.

JOSEPH MOHR, 1818

GOD'S GREATEST GIFT

For God so loved the world that He gave His
only begotten Son, that whoever believes in Him
should not perish but have everlasting life.

Therefore, having been justified by faith,
we have peace with God through our Lord
Jesus Christ.

JOHN 3:16–17; ROMANS 5:1

Christ came into a world that had problems
much like the ones with which we grapple
today. We often imagine that the world to
which Jesus came was not complicated and
that its problems were not complex. But
historians tell us otherwise. They tell us that
the problems of that day were similar to the
problems of our day.

To those without the joy of living, Jesus
said, "I have come that they might have life,
and that they might have it more abundantly"
(John 10:10b).

To those who bore the chafing burden of

the guilt of sin, he said, "Be of good cheer; your sins are forgiven you" (Matthew 9:2b).

To the friendless He said, "I call you not servants…but I have called you friends" (John 15:15 KJV).

Christmas means that Immanuel has come—that God is with us (Matthew 1:23). It means that our sordid, failure-fraught pasts can be defeated and changed by Jesus' sacrifice on the cross and His victorious resurrection. It means that we can be brought into God's family, heirs of God and citizens of Heaven. Christmas means that God comes into the night of our suffering and sorrow, saying, "I am with you always" and, "I will give you rest" (Matthew 28:20; 11:28).

This Christmas season I ask you, Is Christ real to you? Does He actually live in your heart? Has He taken up residence in your life?

Make sure this Christmas of your salvation, by repenting of your sins and asking Christ to come into your life and be your Savior and Lord forever.

O Come All Ye Faithful

O come, all ye faithful,
Joyful and triumphant,
O come ye, O come ye to Bethlehem.
Come and behold Him,
Born the King of Angels!
O come, let us adore Him,
O come, let us adore Him,
O come, let us adore Him,
Christ, the Lord.

Sing, choirs of angels,
Sing in exultation!
Sing, all ye citizens of heaven above!
Glory to God,
all Glory in the highest!
O come, let us adore Him,
O come, let us adore Him,
O come, let us adore Him,
Christ, the Lord.

But You

It isn't your gold or silver,
your talents great or small,
your voice, or your gift of drawing,
or the crowd you go with at all;
it isn't your friends or pastimes,
your looks or your clothes so gay;
it isn't your home or family,
or even the things you say;
it isn't your choice of amusements,
it isn't the life you lead,
it isn't the thing you prize the most,
or the books you like to read;
no, it isn't the things you have, dear,
or the things you like to do,
the Master is searching deeper...
He seeks not yours, but you.

It's your heart that Jesus longs for;
your will to be made His own,
with self on the cross forever,
and Jesus alone on the throne.

RUTH BELL GRAHAM
Collected Poems

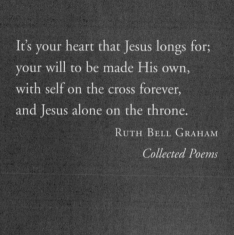

It is our hope that this Advent devotional
has been a blessing to you and your loved ones.
The text was taken in part from *This Christmas Night*
by Billy and Ruth Graham which can be found
in Christian bookstores everywhere.

To order more Advent devotionals,
go to www.thomasnelson.com.